INSIDE SPIDERS

THE LEXI RUDNITSKY FIRST BOOK PRIZE IN POETRY

The Lexi Rudnitsky First Book Prize in Poetry is a collaboration between Persea Books and The Lexi Rudnitsky Poetry Project. It sponsors the annual publication of a poetry collection by an American woman who has yet to publish a full-length book of poems. Lexi Rudnitsky (1972–2005) grew up outside of Boston. She studied at Brown University and Columbia University, where she wrote poetry and cultivated a profound relationship with a lineage of women poets that extends from Muriel Rukeyser to Heather McHugh. Her own poems exhibit both a playful love of language and a fierce conscience. Her writing appeared in *The Antioch Review, Columbia: A Journal of Literature and Art, The Nation, The New Yorker, The Paris Review, Pequod,* and *The Western Humanities Review.* In 2004, she won the Milton Kessler Memorial Prize for Poetry from Harpur Palate. Lexi died suddenly in 2005, just months after the birth of her first child and the acceptance for publication of her first book of poems, *A Doorless Knocking into Night* (Mid-List Press, 2006). The Lexi Rudnitsky First Book Prize in Poetry was founded to memorialize her and to promote the type of poet and poetry in which she so spiritedly believed.

Previous winners of the Lexi Rudnitsky First Book Prize in Poetry:

2012   Allison Seay, *To See the Queen*
2011   Laura Cronk, *Having Been an Accomplice*
2010   Cynthia Marie Hoffman, *Sightseer*
2009   Alexandra Teague, *Mortal Geography*
2008   Tara Bray, *Mistaken for Song*
2007   Anne Shaw, *Undertow*
2006   Alena Hairston, *The Logan Topographies*

INSIDE SPIDERS

poems

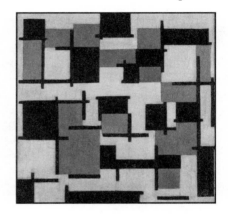

Leslie Shinn

WINNER OF THE LEXI RUDNITSKY FIRST BOOK PRIZE

A Karen & Michael Braziller Book
PERSEA BOOKS / NEW YORK

Persea Books, Inc.
277 Broadway
New York, NY 10007

Library of Congress Cataloging-in-Publication Data
Shinn, Leslie, 1953–
[Poems. Selections]
Inside Spiders : poems / Leslie Shinn.
        pages cm
"A Karen & Michael Braziller Book."
Winner of the Lexi Rudnitsky First Book Prize
ISBN 978-0-89255-439-3 (original trade pbk. : alk. paper) I. Title.
PS3619.H577A6 2014
811'.6—dc23
                        2014002265

Designed by Rita Lascaro
Printed in the United States of America
First Printing

To Hart. To Lily.

Contents

INSIDE SPIDERS

NIGHTINGALE

He had forced flowers—thin,
crenulated bells—tied on the naked stunted
trees of his closed court—enticements—
and when withered, replaced.

Taken to his side as he moved from bed
to chair to table on the porcelain floors,
a perch, unused but ready, its crossed
bars laid with seeds and jewels.

He sat arranged in his dragon dress, and his books
came. The slaves and quiet children
in white robes dragged them to his feet
on old carpets and lifted page over page

while he waited all day unspeaking
the evening custom of the valuable bird that,
plainest gray and held only by air
above the falling crown of sunset,

sang to light the heart's dark lantern.

ARRANGEMENT

Between us, coffee
and the scrim of city air, a cast
off the gleam
of heat, still present.

A poor flower in a plain
vase for me to look at, else.
Then a little talk lifts,
the detail no more etched

than your beautiful stainless
face, and opposite me,
from your place in all this light,

do you become hidden.

COMPLINE

All Saints Convent, Catonsville, Maryland

The thrown arms of the cloister
draw evening's thin sleeve of light
along the nave. Under those black
vaults, high fans scissor and one
candle cup hangs, white sustenance,
tangent to the moon.

Without, the brought dogs soar
on their tethers but the fleet
deer, still hungry, escape. New webs
gleam empty in the lilied fields,
though here with us was that reach met,
and the little hours kept all day to their intervals.

Owls cast from the hunched trees.
Together late, we rich few are full up.

THE GROWN BOY

The fog let in, it breathes
its smoke beneath the shut door
where—dirtcake, scarecat—
he lolls in his bad bed.

The paintings look down
on the piled planes of his bones, the oval
of his face drawn on the pillow,
white on white in the darkened dream as, years on,

and gone from the locked past with his belongings,
he appears again whole, holding my provisional gift:
pomegranate, the meat and seeds
the heart he eats from his knife.

THE RADIO

At table the children,
allowed the radio,
unaccountably chose opera.
The light steadied under the swung lamp,
the cloth clean and pulled over the center,
the music low but building.

Tableau: the palm-sized players,
magnified behind the water glasses,
minuet round the salt.

Any talk was of costumes,
making and remarking their hats and the king
lovely, all along his robes
of decided red were drawn
noble, resting dogs:

what they saw when they heard.

PASSENGER

At your death, mother, the death ornaments
appeared, the held, kicked attendants,
tiny sparrow-dove splayed outside
on the floor, the cracked wing working,
the mystery girl
at the room's edge lofted in smoke
along with *your* mother in torn sepia, who
hid in your grudge-crowded bed.

How you did strive, then,
to kiss what was left of me
when it came to you,

and how you said so evenly,
"Now, don't cry," looking down,

bound for a minute in my own hands,
paler but set in your ways.

RATS

A brace of dead ones
at the foot of the steps,
a present from the neighbor whose
starved dead dog she had patted
and fed. Big, city-basement ones,
poisoned so unmarked, two plump
pouches, their faces finished
where she would not look.
Hole-black! Denser than utmost darkness.
She pushed their small peculiar weights
onto the snow shovel, the terrible tails
writhing senselessly down into the shiny black
bag, the tying shut difficult too.

Streaming clouds, the late sun less
than the lights on next door, she backed
up against her own house, threshold
above cellar and gutter.
Afraid to stay out, afraid to go in.

DROWNED

i.
The whales and fishes were left,
and fine, tasting the trees,
threading through high windows
over tables and beds. Except
they were chased and eaten,
they lived on, chasing and eating.

ii.
Other vultures than the pair, glossy
from the last gulls, paced
and screamed on the bulkheads,
and fell away, but more than two
sparrows splintered inside
and shot the dark length.

iii.
Clouds for light
as the water closed.
A box of glazed paper was fitted
for me in the highest hold, where the snakes
piled and pulsed, where the wildest birds were shelved.
Ground glass my sand and swallow.

iv.
Spiders, uncounted and everyplace, watched, chased,
and wrung in string whole species of unparceled insects.

v.
Halcyon dove alight
over the deepened shores,
the seaming rivers,
my fellow, mate became.
Later, with Rome begun
and again unforgiven,

the sky open clear to the planets,
night after night disappeared.

PLACE

Street set: at seven,
the same grid of slate and grit
with some rain down

through the trees, those mercies.

But left and deep under the shaken leaves
the revenant dark lies and keeps
its limbs and long wings,
its hidden heads that watch

me, under my jacked umbrella,
move back in with the dog.

HOUSEWIFE

When the spiders come
inside, surprised off
the cacti that summered out,

and string up the ceiling,
and lace the white curtain
across in the scant light,

the beauties, I breathe them down.
Unpinned, they fall
into my fine-lipped cup,

the paper lid on
through the whole house
to the sunk garden,

the hopes handed out, and staying out.

PROCESSION

Music is drawn up the street.
The singing and instruments arrive
and pass not louder, much,

nor more distinct. Thin rain.
The saints and more than one
Mary pitch on palanquins held

by boys struggling with attention.
The girls, candles. Mothers frown
at the smiles and loft babies in doll clothes.

More rain sweeps this green hall,
the trees, the windows rinsed.

CONTENTS

The collector lifts the ceiling lid,
the two streetside trees lean in
and brush the walls and desks.
A few tiles crumble while the soft-
looking fans look back and forth.

Composed, eyes inward, he thinks to cut
from the books what he wants,
the title sheets veils over
the columns, the columns running down.
Easy, he picks up and puts down
a vase, the encased drawings
and photographs, then
leaves all of it, the sky again
at the windows, cloud and sun
uncaught, riches and riches.

THE LITTLE QUEENS

after Lisbeth Zwerger

i.

Archaic throne, back double high
and the seat long as if folded out,
a viney plush marked in little
hook-nubbled birds, the nubs
the eyes and gnarled feet. More birds:
two dinosaur ones with torn skin
keep guard on the chair's top
over the sleeping child, their tail
feathers curled in a coil.

She sleeps, one black sash of lashes
lifts, and up seeps the background,
brown purples mottled to marble
at the chair arms. Her arms covered
in quivering stripes still on her lap, laid
with roses on watered silk. The ladies-in-waiting,
tiny little girls, fold to a screen at her side
and murmur their fear of the peahen come,
strutting and clapping her beak.

ii.

Chased and stopped
at the mud pool,
all see
the drowned doll on top
of the water, ties untied,
its dear dress

of reddest hearts
run to white.

iii.

We try on hats.
A saw-cut crown
with paint jewels,
a cap and bells
and sun and rain ones
stick from the soft
gray box of old spreads
and cloaks. Helmet
of Mercury, wings
sewn of leaves
and a dusky cone
lit with dull stars.

You choose one
with a fiery spray
and from under, a crescent
of your face shows,
plain of temple over
plane of cheek,
the eye cornered
and pared by shadows
from the windows, miles up.

Under our skin shoes
the floor pours and pours.

NIGHT AIR

Night cure. Solvent vapors
and orbs streamed and spun
under the cut moon.

Astir, lower,
the white air
lapped at the walks

and reached the trees'
spurred limbs.

My ghost moved on the lawn
with a little smoke
blowing round him,

his unshown hand
proof against the black
fence and concrete

my signal
when I passed him by cold in the car.

THE VISIT

Elaborate directions sent
and later elaborations telephoned.
Arm-waving imagined, almost audible,
and fine finger adjustments
that draw the street
a little more to the left
after the sign,
that paint the house a green
I can see from where I am,
early on the Tuesday before.

And the window I see,
its glass clean and dark and showing
the bird's cage near, and the clean, dark little table,
with you close up wrapped in your gift cardigan,
all the edges roses.

THE TWO DAYS

She missed streets and turns with signature
inattention. The lavish little park, reached by each of them
through full circles, cost to stay in, cost to leave.

At and after the restaurant, she noted and dismissed
the low clouds, the lines of trees,
her lovely long hand with its heavy ring

swept, then shut, all their talk
into the worn candy box
of their old conversations and letters.

Sparrows everywhere that second
evening in the same place.
White flowers folded up against the fence.

Nothing invited, nothing merited
closer regard or further question.
Honey cake, coffee—the same in any

weather, the two of them.

NORTH SIXTH

Sun opens the sidewalk
and the wind, a music:
the bell's a bottle's roll,
the rattles and claps
a remnant leaf walking by

the place two men sit
before a torn painting
of wires and vines. Each holds
a bowl of all they get today
under one blooming tree
that hands out its white cupped plates.

The lot's a poor city
field, the trash the deep
generic mix of metals and glass,
caged dogs and the ratty birds
watching as now, over the broken
houses, the light comes up
hard as it can go.

TRAP

Anymore, it's a fright at first light,
the ascetic white square of the kitchen lifting
in the windows' cold rain or dark shine.

Away go the bugs in a black scuttle,
and the mouse's gnawn body is dispatched quick,
flat and stiff, as you've seen yourself.

Bring in the flowers! The fine white roses or the palm
of clover heads that float in the bowl near my cup
in these mornings near winter, when death is a good start.

COVER

Full black river bowl
deep below. At the rim,
where some trees stand around,
the sky's china-figured lid fits over.

Parapet.
A short list of pigeons
tips foot to foot
when his bald face swivels near.

He leans his knees into the low
wall and sees the current
push and fold
and shut over the bank,

the day drowned,
the sun removed.

TAKING PILLS

Lethe, nothing!
A half-dose and chase
to that pressed sleep,
the draped form shaped
under the slid shutter
and gone till the fish-up
from the scraped barrel,
out of that black swim.

SKIT

Bare and white
a sheet of wall
between two windows.
Along a passage,

I watch from across,
and a girl that color is there.
Pared glance.
All day the light evening.

ELEVATOR

With neither eye
I know the ineluctable
drop of your shoulder
against the wall of our small
interior. Our bodies beside
one another, I align my legs
a way I play they'd fit yours,
then think my breath along
your hidden, birdwing clavicle.
I raise my chin a little away
from having my tongue over
your magnificent scar when the doors
hiss and part, and I step onto
the flush floor, my back naked,
as I suppose, of any notice.

A SPIDER

Pendulum, diadem,
a dark bauble loose
and undulate in his sloop,
his sheet, pinned as it is

at the glass and the sash
where I kneel, postulant,
to fix him, his fixed, taut
gauntlet and his thready legs.

I keep, as the light leans down, note
of his stays and his drift, and have his
drawn map now to draw to mine—
considered, resolute, and fine.

BABY OWL

Held for a while, it relaxed,
expanded. The tree birds gaped,
the tethered ones wrenched to see it,
the men at the strings whispered, shifted form.

The hill swerved around, the place
where the sidewalk began blurred,
my feet and the long feathers swirling.
A thick muff my gloved hands
at the poor bird's wide throat,
my coat and my yellow eyes
closed under the moon's thin paring.

SWEEP

Halved and halved
again, then torn through
your sharp fingers, my letter,
the letter sent to me.

The white pieces rain
and ash below our eyes, lips still.
The room a circle,
the light that shape.

I DREAMED A RAT AND FOX

i.
A pretty tea was laid.
The rat reposed
in comfortable coil
upon an elegant striped
saucer at my elbow, his fine,
chiseling teeth visible in his
charming smile.

He leaned companionably,
the talk being of past meals.

Soon I began to feel quite tired—
too warm from the drink, and full of sweets—
and felt a little critical then, noticing
how, as he reached with blessed
appetite for yet another something,
and his sleeve pulled back,

a few fleas clung shining to his foreleg.

ii.
Pile of pitch and ailanthus tree a silhouette
against the lit house, and a little fox
met me there in her coat
that was gray at her head and red at the rest of her.

She gave her dainty
and pointy face to me,
dancing up
on her legs in whole turns
that swept memory
under episode till she leaped

and surprise, I came away clean.

ACTUAL FICTION

Any story, any, I put
and think myself into, protagonist,
pro, tag, a made-up textual real real girl.

If, too, there's a slide, a transparency,
sidelong glimpse-snap of a man
slouched, mouth open, unaware as unobserved,
half-seen half-out of a car window,
car going by what seems like pretty

fast   then, ever helpful, keen to lend meaning, I dream up my fit
in the photograph,

and I—

in a coat I had in college, a blue dark
as the night I am also driving, the slice,

the piece,
the rubbed oval
of my poor face
flattened by the proximity,

showing my teeth—

become the whole book and the cover.

AUBADE

Jupiter! My first look
over the frieze of stars,
past radium Io
to the mythical vapors,
the liquid defiles, in a roil
synchronous with the heart's waters,
the ruins flinging and breathing.
When the acetylene moons
slid magnetic back,
the roofs came up,

and the fleeting mists
rose in a rain of light.

STORES

His savings seen
at the lot's rough edge:
bricks and rocks, mirror shards
in sharp piles, old linoleum rolled,
tied tight and standing for pillars
around his cup, his many bottles
unfilled and unemptied,
and his papers, a worn stack
worried in and out of his coat.

Untired, he enacts arrangement.
Borders inch, the room roomier
or shrunk, ever tidy, as he leans
lean over his miracles of coffee and grub,
his burred blanket laid square
under the ordered stars.

STATION

The long box
of the corridor,
notched with doors,
he stalks over and over
down to her small room
only to try, as he passes
as if in wrath,
to find her eyes with his,
iris and pupil, the same ink.

Today, no.
She finds the floor, the wall
as he nears, or stands looking out
at the streets, green and grey,
night looking in.

BACK GARDEN

I see it
that no one comes in,
flat and foreshortened
with the spikes up
everywhere, the one tree.
A privet like a hat
and the ivy strands
where, later as before,
a few roses will rust.

I keep it swept, and like
to rest in one of the chairs
pulled out of the sun.
Here behind the deep house,
sided by deeper houses, I watch
the light draw an edge
and jump over it, as the clear wall
rises above the fence, the limit
learned—no, loved
and sought.

THINGS BROKE

Things broke at that altitude,
the fever up bright
for days, the ceiling mosaic
pocked and unpieced,
the raindown splinters lay
in your hair where you lay

in shock and savor.
Who knows who was consulted,
the whole room tipped and strewn,
undraped. All shiny, ruby,
the rafter devil swings
his little legs and laughs
through the burned years, broken
at that amplitude, his crying life.

THREE

arms

the baby has

beneath
a countenance clear of shadow

one right

and of the two

left

one's hand is

the pearl clench of

        a new peony

and one's

two bone fingers
a small scissors

      the fresh bud
         or fold of rose paper

which will flourish
and be saved

THE TEST

The building opposite
so ornate it nearly draws
his attention from his room,
empty and familiar, a graph line
of low table, spiked door,
and a risen bed where, loaded
with lead and covered by his
mother's eyes, he waits for
the colorless illustrations
they can only see, and no one face.

The day divides. Mosaic
shadow below the rough curtain,
the sun moving off to one side.

SMALL TREES IN SNOW

Two narrow rows
of ten, a child's
allee, thin boughs
swung with the red
bead fruits, pretty
swags that catch, too,
the sparrows who
dive in brief arcs.
The day tapers
to night enough
for these flung stars,
a fine thousand.

AMPHITHEATER

No curtain. The stage juts
under lamps that also color the wings in grays.
Moths descriptive under this propped lid of light,
flying their black shadows. A table and chairs.
It's a mystery, and we watch
from our blankets, learning its tracery to logic,
avid for the game's hand, as it hides the knife
and tips us a little from the cool spoon of artifice.
Full, this summer night. Still.
A breeze now, as the trees take their places again
and we move away to find all our dark houses.

AT THE BALLET

The theater's constellation
chandelier beamed a piece
of your profile in silver
over the other half-moons
and matches of starched cuffs

and jewels. After the interval,
high hidden lamps kindled
the stage variously: white boxes
brought from the deep wings, or color-fan
oblongs into which the dancers stepped

in class clothes: black pink white.
Their arced lines and flown breath
shot a light caught rows and rows
back where, in your dark lap,
the heart in your hands lay quiet.

"LITTLE HOBBIN"

after Theodor Storm

This room the whole night
and baby Hobbin unhappy awake,
his mother's dress a drape
clung to, black and blown over
his midnight eyes. The close length
gathers and slips

off the high bed, down the far floor . . .
Stars above! His harried mother
holds Hobbin, his gown a bell lamp,
his lovely white face
a misery. Or she pushes him
in his pretty pram to and fro,

those shocked dolls
stiff on the pillow.
O Hobbin, sleep, sleep,
her long hands a quiet book
to show you how, apart
from all the clouds racing,

the moon stays still in the fading sky.

AQUARIUM

After Christmas, for ornament,
we culled the toybox bottom
with all our hands, sifting the doll
shoes and kit pieces for the marbles
that clicked in the water with
the two new pretty fishes.

And we let go a snail that way too.
Dropped, he scudded along a little
and rested on his side in the lit water
—we were sure he was dead—
for about two days.

A lemon snail, interesting acid shell,
his flesh a dismaying textural pink,
I admit we coaxed him but gently with a straw
and moved him, still in-turned, closed and deep,
we monitored our new pet's sleep.

The few minutes he turned about became focal.
We memorized his mouth and timorous plastic
antennae and his habit of whole rest, to follow then
what he wanted closely, closely, his beautiful
skirts dragging ruffling against the green glass,
until it was what he had.

SÉANCE

Automatic song edged round
the marked table—scattered
thinly with candlesticks, peeled
cupcakes, and cold tea in her
gold lily set—and a scarf
of light took over her head,
read the automatic drawings
on the smoke silk walls.

Pure dark at the bowed windows.
The air pressed close at the door
that time put between us
and pulled, she then the mirror
where I walked by myself.

DRESSED

Now the jewels.
The pearls vined round
the slant, stemmed path

are chalk stones down
the narrow garden,
a bench the crescent

brow widened white
below diamonds and an old, smooth,
stone-silvered wrap of wall.

        Of the evening, these
dark rich remnants—painted paper lake
of gilded folds laid straight,

the gowned hills
on hidden feet
late coming light.

GARDEN PHOTOGRAPH

The boy looks away
from roses in uncut sheaves,
the white foxgloves' roomettes poised
over leaves in fabulous pagodas.

A few yew stars point from the felt
backdrop. Narrow corner,
shoulder edge, limbs.
Strewn bricks, the wall's leaves

a yellow that is white.
What light lay here. A cut
of grassy cheek, spider eye,
his lips apart.

IN THE SIDE YARD

Mockingbirds come for these
lush fluorescent berries

set naked on stems above bowed
flowers the bees can still find.

The sky is shut into a long box
atop the next house,

its black windows' few curtains chewed to lace.
Down here is a pan for water, no water,

a tongue-scoured bowl,
and the big dog kept short

where its ken lengthens out
only one missing board's width

to the walk, where a tree shakes,
and the shadows pass, darker than dark.

GLANCE

The first
so beguiling
easy as light
a curtain folded
back for the flood

or the flash of the pane dark and clean
from the street that invites past
the strewn chairs and possessions
with the floor pouring out
under everything all of it

DAUGHTER

Long for seven,
her fingers even the papers,
make a ruffle of them and,
when the mother comes,
have snapped her sweater wrong

along the sheath of her,
the pearl knit of her, the silk and skeleton.

Over the bridge home,
she has the necklace she likes,
the city's glitter rings of lights

a scalloped net loose around
her mother, the water
far and dark, a cast, a lace
of collected light

that shimmers what of her mother's
face she can see, what she is shown,
as the moon leans, now, over her head,
and the stars beginning.

NIGHT HOUSE

i.
The grey paper
sky cracks scarily
and bleeds where it folds down
across fields, behind
the grand house
the cab has finally reached.
Here is the older dog
drawn off his pillow, and his
toothless bark.

ii.
Zigzag
checkerboard the roof
and down plainest walls
a salad of thistles mixes through
the mud to the car.

iii.
A figure keeps
at the phosphor window.
Without, the lawn
rolls close and away.

SELF-PORTRAIT

I will make a dress,
ink blue, a lopped triangle
that has as its point
the neck opening, below,
black stick legs
and black shoebox feet.
Armless, and what background
will be seen, for I will
blacken out most of it
a way I like, will be the usual
highs and lows, stars and mud,
or if possible a gray rain color
undivided over some roses,
any horizon line way off, unthought,
in fact above the paper.

IN THE THRONE ROOM KITCHEN

Live dice, the two bees
tumbling in the white window

under the watery green
ceiling, way over the table

where the giant sits in the one chair.
He's wrapped his poor feet in doused wool

same as his toothache rag, his red brick jaw
swathed in liniment up to a rabbity topknot.

Down the long, dark kitchen
those bees are the big noise

now that his head has quieted
and the supper creatures have cooked—

furled black flowers at the ends of arms,
the tails curled close.

With bread and meat measured,
the done day too is counted and marked,

its throw of cloud beheld, its lot of sun.
The chances of its share and want,

enough. The bees cease, and
the night folds in from all sides.

NATIVITY

He'd stepped back. Slant
walls closed them under the roof
cliff, and across the sloped floor

two mendicant dogs slept watchful,
warm in the cold together near
the packed cases, the hard bed.

Below the light bulb star
in her dried-blood-red dress
she held the milky baby

apart from the visitors, their useless gifts.
Some sky and a piece of tree
at the window, the air ice over

the nearing river, the golden companies out
in the silver streets, the ancient dark
deep on the stair and still, still the world.

Acknowledgements

Thanks to the editors of the following journals, in which the poems indicated first appeared.

Agenda (UK): Nightingale
American Writing: Back Garden
Beloit Poetry Journal: The Radio, Séance
The Cortland Review: Drowned, "Little Hobbin"
Disquieting Muses Quarterly Review: A Spider, Arrangement
Ekphrasis: Nativity
Folio: Amphitheater
Phoebe: Compline, The Grown Boy
Salt River Review: North Sixth, Self-Portrait
Tattoo Highway: In the Throne Room Kitchen

"Three" appeared in *Poem, Revised: 54 Poems, Revisions, Discussion* by Robert Hartwell Fiske and Laura Cherry (Marion Street Press, 2008).

Thank you, Gabriel Fried and everyone at Persea Books. Thanks to my teachers, Ellen Bryant Voigt, David Baker, Kathleen Peirce, Chris Forhan. I am ever the richer for the kindness and encouragement I received from the late Almitra David and the late Renate Wood. For the unending inspiration I find in her work, I am indebted to artist Lisbeth Zwerger. Thank you, Susan Kan. Love and gratitude to my round robin, that valuable bird: Jannett Highfill, Diane Gilliam, and Laura Cherry, darling constant.